Magnets

by Karen Latchana Kenney

amicus
readers

1

Amicus Readers are published by Amicus
P.O. Box 1329, Mankato, Minnesota 56002

Printed in the United States of America at Corporate Graphics, North Mankato, Minnesota.

Library of Congress Cataloging-in-Publication Data
Kenney, Karen Latchana.
   Magnets / by Karen Latchana Kenney.
      p. cm. -- (Amicus readers. Everyday science)
   Summary: "Describes how magnets work and gives examples of everyday uses of
magnets. Includes experiments"-- Provided by publisher.
   Includes index.
   ISBN 978-1-60753-019-0 (lib. bdg.)
   1. Magnets--Juvenile literature. 2. Magnets--Experiments--Juvenile literature. I. Title.
   QC757.5.K46 2011
   538'.4--dc22
                            2010011282

Series Editor   Rebecca Glaser
Series Designer   Mary Herrmann
Production Designer   Bobbi J. Wyss
Photo Researcher   Heather Dreisbach

Photo Credits
Apple Tree House/Getty Images, 9; Dan Van Den Broeke/Dreamstime.
com, 12, 21 (b); David R. Frazier Photolibrary, Inc./Alamy, 13; flashfilm/
Getty Images, 5; Hans Weißer/dpa/Corbis, 17, 20 (m); Javier Larrea/
Photolibrary, 11, 20 (b); Jeffrey Coolidge/Getty Images, 6, 20
(t); Jianghongyan/Dreamstime.com, 21 (t); Jim Wileman/Alamy,
cover; Michael Chamberlin/Shutterstock, 7, 21 (m); Olga Khorkova/
Dreamstime.com, 19; Peter Albrektsen/iStockphoto, 8; Raul Touzon/
Getty Images, 1; Thomas Hottner/iStockphoto, 16; Tommounsey/
iStockphoto, 10, 20 (t); YOSHIKAZU TSUNO/AFP/Getty Images, 15

1222
42010

10 9 8 7 6 5 4 3 2 1

Table of Contents

Liam's toy train connects with magnets.

He pulls it along its track.

We use magnets to pull or push things.

Magnets have a force that pushes or pulls.

This force makes magnets stick to metal.

It is strongest at two ends.

They are the north and south poles.

force

Jill shuts the refrigerator door.

Magnets keep the door closed.

Their north and south poles pull together.

poles

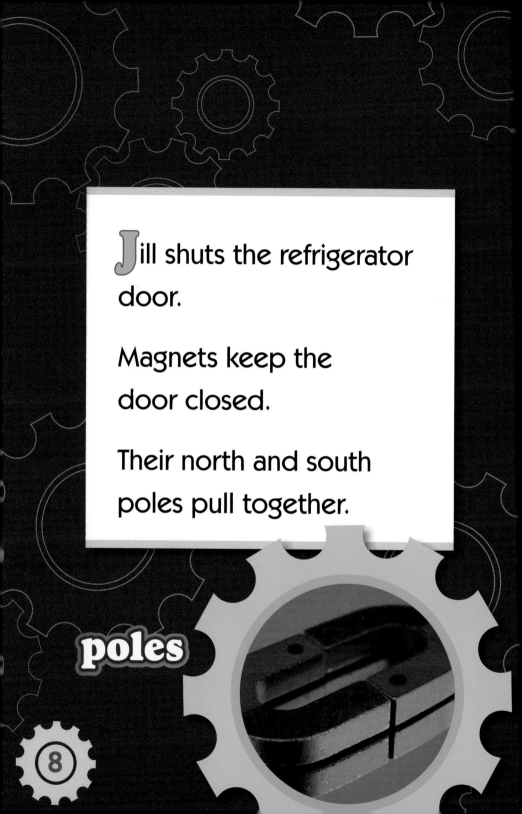

Nick builds a cool shape with his toy.

The parts stick together.

They are magnetic.

magnetic

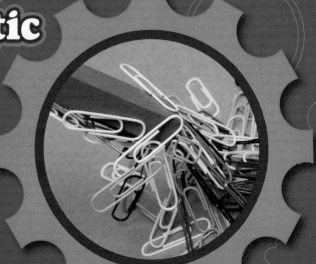

A big magnet hangs over trash at the recycling center.

It pulls metal from the trash.

recycling center

13

When two north poles try to touch, magnets push away.

The force makes things float.

See how magnets make this fish float?

The fast maglev train floats above its track.

Magnets in the train and the track push away from each other.

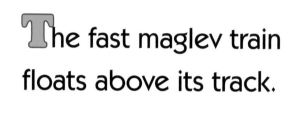

maglev train

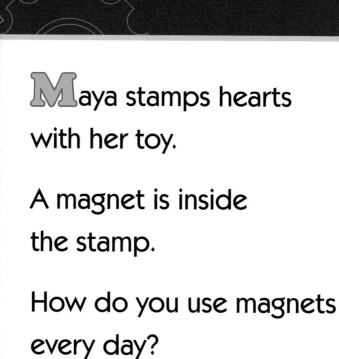

Maya stamps hearts with her toy.

A magnet is inside the stamp.

How do you use magnets every day?

Picture Glossary

force—something that changes the movement of an object; Magnetic force pulls some metals to magnets.

maglev train—a train that uses magnets to float above and move along a track

magnetic—being able to attract iron, steel, or other magnets

metal—a hard, shiny material such as iron or steel

poles—two points or sides of a magnet that have force

recycling center—a place where metal, paper, and plastic are sorted and made into things that can be used again

21

Ideas for Parents and Teachers

Science and technology aren't just for engineers—we use them every day. *Everyday Science,* an Amicus Readers Level 1 series, introduces children to scientific concepts through familiar situations and objects. The picture glossary and photo labels reinforce new vocabulary. Use the following strategies to help your children predict, read, and comprehend.

Before Reading
- Ask students to look through the photographs in the book. Tell them to ask questions about the photographs.
- Read the title aloud to students. Ask them to make predictions of what the book will tell them about magnets.
- Discuss what students already know about magnets. Then discuss what they would like to know about magnets. Write answers on the board.

Read the Book
- Read the book to the children, or have them read independently.
- Ask students to note the glossary words while they are reading. Challenge them to guess the meanings before they read the glossary definitions.

After Reading
- Have the children check their guesses against the glossary definitions on pages 20–21.
- Try the simple activities on page 23.
- Prompt the children to think more, asking questions such as: *Why are the ends of a magnet called poles? Can you always see magnets or are some inside objects or machines?*

Experimenting with Magnets

Try This:

1. Stick two button magnets together. Now flip one magnet and try to stick them together again. Did it work?

2. Put metal paperclips, aluminum foil, and a soda can on a table. Put a magnet near each object. Do they all stick to the magnet?

3. Put a steel washer on a thin piece of cardboard. Put a strong bar magnet under the cardboard. Does the magnet move the washer?

What happened?

1. No. The poles are the same and the magnets push apart from each other.

2. No. The paperclips pull to the magnet. The foil and soda can do not. They are not magnetic.

3. Yes. The force of the magnet is strong. It moves through the cardboard and pulls the washer.

Index

Web Sites

BBC KS2 Bitesize: Science – Physical processes. Magnets and Springs.
http://www.bbc.co.uk/schools/ks2bitesize/science/physical_processes/

BrainPop! Magnetism.
http://www.brainpop.com/science/motionsforcesandtime/magnetism/preview.weml

Creative Kids at Home. Magnets.
http://www.creativekidsathome.com/science/magnet.html

Nasa's Kids Science News Network. Why Do Magnets Work? video
http://ksnn.larc.nasa.gov/k2/s_magnetsWork_v.html